MW01131400

IMAGES
of America

FRENCH LICK
AND WEST
BADEN SPRINGS

"In Xanadu did Kubla Khan, A stately pleasure-dome decree," wrote Samuel Taylor Coleridge in *Kubla Khan* in 1816. The "pleasure dome" was not looking too stately when first visited by the author in the late 1980s. The once magnificent West Baden Springs Hotel was all but abandoned to the elements, looking more like the deserted Xanadu of *Citizen Kane* than the one described by Coleridge in *Kubla Khan*. The last guests had checked out during the Great Depression over 50 years earlier. Since then, inhabitants have included Jesuit priests, college students, and a colony of stray cats. The near demise and ultimate rebirth of this remarkable structure is but one storyline in the fascinating history of French Lick–West Baden. (Courtesy of French Lick West Baden Museum.)

ON THE COVER: The magnificent domed atrium of the West Baden Springs Hotel was instantly hailed as the "Eighth Wonder of the World" when it opened in 1902. Along with the elegant French Lick Hotel, nine area casinos, and other assorted hotels and clubs, they formed a vibrant resort destination that attracted visitors from all over the world to this secluded corner of Indiana. (Courtesy of French Lick West Baden Museum.)

IMAGES
of America

FRENCH LICK
AND WEST
BADEN SPRINGS

Jerry Copas

ARCADIA
PUBLISHING

Published by Arcadia Publishing
Charleston, South Carolina

Library of Congress Control Number: 2018947604

For all general information, please contact Arcadia Publishing:
Telephone 843-853-2070
Fax 843-853-0044
E-mail sales@arcadiapublishing.com
For customer service and orders:
Toll-Free 1-888-313-2665

Visit us on the Internet at www.arcadiapublishing.com

*To my loving wife Kathy, for her support and patience, as
I indulge in my ambitions of becoming an author!*

CONTENTS

ACKNOWLEDGMENTS

Many people have helped with the production of this book, sharing with me their photographs and memories of the French Lick and West Baden communities. First and foremost, my heartfelt thanks and sincerest gratitude go out to Patty Drabing and the staff of the superb French Lick West Baden Museum. Patty's love of history and dedication to preservation have helped to make the museum a showplace for the community and an invaluable resource. I learned so much in the many hours I spent doing research in the museum. Patty was always there to help with facts, anecdotes, and access to the archived treasures lovingly preserved in this outstanding facility. I highly recommend visitors stop by the museum and indulge for a few hours in the rich history on display there.

Many thanks to the French Lick Resort and its generous access to the company's historic archives. Steve Rondinaro and his staff in the marketing department are dedicated stewards for the rich history of the resort. They do a splendid job preserving the legacy of elegance and tradition that guests have experienced there for more than 100 years. Resort historian Jeff Lane is a walking encyclopedia of dates, facts, and stories. Discussing history with him is indeed a privilege. It is clear that heritage and history are important to the resort's owners, since they have such talented and knowledgeable people working for them.

I so enjoyed meeting Suzanne Emmons and hearing her recollections of the area's history. She provided me with some key images that helped to make this book complete. And lastly, my sincere thanks and admiration go out to Robin Coulter. She is passionate about preserving the history of the Springs Valley, and her superb Facebook group is a deep well of facts, dates, and recollections. Her generous assistance with fact-finding and proofreading insured this book would be accurate and concise.

INTRODUCTION

It was a cold and snowy afternoon in the late 1980s when I first visited the historic West Baden Springs Hotel. Having grown up in Southern Indiana, I had heard stories of an abandoned and derelict luxury resort hidden away in the rugged hills of Orange County. So, with a youthful zeal for adventure and casual disregard of trespass law, my friends and I set out to locate this mythical place. I will never forget my first sight of this marvelous structure on that day. Through the faded and peeling archway, the imposing landmark was set against the dark woods like some kind of forgotten temple. Framed by bare trees swaying in the winter wind, there were no lights, no people, not a sign of life anywhere. The once grand avenue leading up to the main entrance was cracked and crumbling. Broken trees and limbs lay strewn about. Dead leaves blew across the cracked cobblestones. Overgrown vines and weeds choked the once lush gardens that had not been tended for years. Surprised to find an unlocked door, my companions and I crept inside the old hotel. Through a dark hallway, we emerged into the magnificent domed atrium. I stood in awe, speechless at the tarnished elegance. The smells of mold and decay added to the melancholy spectacle. We spoke in hushed tones, as if not to awaken the spirits residing there. Water could be heard dripping somewhere, as our ears strained for sounds of life. I detected movement in a nearby corridor and was surprised to find that feral cats had taken up residence in the place. They were the only guests remaining in this forgotten palace that had once hosted movie stars, gangsters, and the wealthy titans of American industry. Closing my eyes, I could imagine the place filled with crowds of elegant ladies and dapper gentlemen, dressed in the styles of the early 20th century and waltzing to the music of a chamber orchestra. Uniformed bellmen darting here and there, shuttling carpetbags and steamer trunks and serving guests from all over the world. Waiters with silver trays offering crystal glasses filled with "Sprudel Water," the legendary elixir that promised to cure all ills. But on this dismal winter day, the place belonged to a few stray cats. After exploring the dim hallways, the late afternoon daylight began to fade, and the gloomy solitude of the place became overwhelming. My companions and I departed, filled with more questions than answers. How did this crumbling marvel ever come to be here? Why was it built? What was the attraction to this isolated corner of rural Indiana? And how did it come to reach such a sad state of ruin? Could this amazing landmark ever be saved and returned to the glory and opulence of its heyday?

My questions from that day have instilled in me a lifelong fascination of the French Lick–West Baden region, known collectively as the Springs Valley. The combined histories of these communities are indeed compelling, filled with tales of exploration, ambition, greed, philanthropy, and the promised miracles of a foul-smelling water that magically seeps from the ground. In ancient times, generations of Native Americans were drawn here in pursuit of the buffalo herds. The great animals were attracted to exposed salt licks produced by the mineral springs. Today's modern visitors come here seeking the perfect round of golf or a winning hand at the poker table. Fortunes have been won and lost by wealthy investors and speculators who sought riches in the development of the valley. Simple wooden inns and way stations were transitioned into luxurious hotels. The pungent water has been extracted, bottled, and branded, then shipped all over the world as a cure for everything from dysentery to diabetes. Up to a dozen trains a day brought visitors from near and far to "take the waters" and restore their health with a variety of outdoor activities. Horseback riding, skeet shooting, swimming, and bowling were among the recreations guests could choose from. For bicycling enthusiasts, there was a one-of-a-kind, double-decker, wooden riding track. This structure provided cyclists a one-third mile loop, covered from the weather, with a track for horses and pony carts on its lower level. Illegal gambling flourished in the region, as authorities turned a blind eye. Gangsters and criminals have found refuge here, staying one step ahead of the law in this secluded corner of Indiana. Ironically, in the 1990s it was the appeal of state-approved, legal gambling that would become a modern-day salvation to the valley's economic ills.

Today, the once crumbling West Baden Springs Hotel has been rescued and lovingly renovated to its former glory. Together with the completely restored French Lick Hotel, the two legendary properties make up a thriving resort that is once again attracting visitors from all over the world. Two historic golf courses have been restored, and a new one has been added. This completely new course, created by noted designer Pete Dye, has been heralded by professional golfers worldwide for its beauty and challenging play. Major Professional Golfers' Association (PGA) tournaments are held on the course, showcasing this area to a worldwide audience like never before. A recent expansion at the French Lick Hotel added 58,000 square feet of conference and event space. And high-stakes casino gambling has returned to the valley, all perfectly legal this time, in a 42,000-square-foot facility featuring 1,200 slot machines and 46 gaming tables. The dubious qualities of the "healing waters" have long since been dispelled; their appeal is now just a curious footnote in the history of the Springs Valley.

The restoration and salvation of these communities is inspiring and a monument to a notable Indiana philanthropist, the late Bill Cook. His forethought and love of history provided the spark that helped return French Lick and West Baden to the list of the world's finest resorts. The story of the rise and fall of fortunes in this valley indeed has a happy ending. I hope you will enjoy reading about this rich history as much as I have enjoyed writing about it.

—Jerry Copas

One

EARLY HISTORY OF THE SPRINGS VALLEY

The American bison had a profound effect on early human activity in the area that was to become Southern Indiana. Millions of these great beasts migrated through the region, crossing the Ohio River near the falls at Louisville and continuing northwest to ford the Wabash River near present-day Vincennes. Years of stomping and grazing created a beaten-down path that became known as the "Buffalo Trace." This primitive track was 10 to 20 feet wide in places, creating a crude highway through the wilderness. The paths often converged around exposed mineral deposits called salt licks, which occurred near natural springs. The bison were attracted to these features, as were deer, bears, foxes, and other wildlife. These areas were bountiful hunting grounds for the Native American tribes in the region as well as early trappers and explorers. In 1792, a missionary reported seeing a rather large buffalo salt lick several acres in size near what would eventually become the French Lick settlement. Revolutionary war hero George Rogers Clark is often credited with naming the area French Lick, after the French trappers and explorers he encountered there.

Soon, the old buffalo trace was suitable for wagon travel, and the traffic increased. Small inns and way stations popped up along the trail, providing food and comfort to the weary travelers. A stockade was built near the French Lick settlement, to protect early settlers from frequent Indian raids. Dr. William Bowles built a small inn on the site of the present French Lick Springs Hotel around 1845. The structure was not luxurious by any means; it was an all-wooden building offering simple rooms and hearty meals. But Bowles was convinced the water from the mineral springs possessed curative healing powers, and he began to serve the product to his guests. Dr. John Lane, a former business associate of Dr. Bowles, soon built his own wooden-frame hotel a mile or so north of Bowles's French Lick Springs Hotel, in 1855. He initially named his place the Mile Lick Inn but soon changed the name to West Baden Inn, after the famous Wiesbaden Spa in Germany. Dr. Lane also recognized the potential demand for the mineral water and its alleged medicinal qualities.

As travel through the region increased, the two hotels began a rivalry that would endure for decades and result in a resort community that would become known worldwide.

The American bison created the first trail into the French Lick–West Baden area, forging a migratory path through the future state of Indiana from the Ohio River near Louisville to the Wabash River near Vincennes. The creatures were drawn to the exposed mineral deposits or salt licks produced by the region's natural springs. Native American tribes and early pioneers found good hunting near the springs, establishing encampments and outposts for traders and trappers. (Courtesy of French Lick West Baden Museum.)

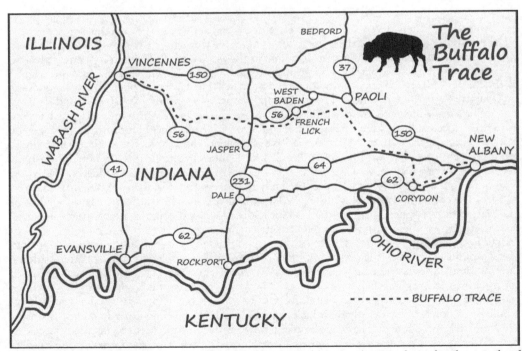

The Buffalo Trace carved an early path through the wilderness, beaten down by thousands of hoofprints as the beasts migrated between seasonal feeding grounds. The herds forded the Ohio River near the falls at present-day Louisville and crossed the Wabash River near Vincennes bound for the grazing lands on the Illinois prairie. The path was broad and flat in most places, providing a natural trail for settlers, explorers, and military personnel. (Author's collection.)

GEORGE ROGERS CLARK.

A Revolutionary War hero, Gen. George Rogers Clark often gets credit for naming the French Lick region. While traveling the Buffalo Trace in the late 1700s, he evidently encountered French traders encamped near the salt licks. Some traditions insist the French once claimed ownership of the springs area, having been bestowed the land by the Piankeshaw tribe in 1742. (Courtesy of French Lick West Baden Museum.)

Dr. William Bowles opened the first hotel at French Lick sometime around 1845. Descended from a long line of physicians, Bowles was described by his contemporaries as handsome, charismatic, and deeply religious. However, as a young physician in Fredericksburg, Indiana, in 1820, he was convicted of grave robbing, a practice not uncommon among physicians of those days who needed cadavers for dissection. (Courtesy of French Lick West Baden Museum.)

This is Dr. William Bowles's first hotel at French Lick, opened sometime around the spring of 1845. This very simple wooden-frame structure was not luxurious by any means. It offered only the most basic lodging and meals and provided a welcome rest for guests weary from the challenges of traversing the wilderness. This original, humble roadhouse provided the footprint for what will become the elegant and luxurious French Lick Springs Hotel. (Both, courtesy of French Lick West Baden Museum.)

This is the original wooden hotel at West Baden. It was built by Dr. John Lane, a former business associate of Dr. Bowles. Lane's tenure at the French Lick Hotel resulted in a disagreement with Bowles. Lane departed, built a new hotel one mile north, and named it the Mile Lick Inn. This created a competition that would endure for decades and result in two world-class resorts. Lane's hotel soon expanded, and he changed the name to West Baden. No known photographs exist of Dr. Lane. (Courtesy of French Lick West Baden Museum.)

Two

A RESORT IS BORN

The end of the 19th century brought significant changes to Indiana's Springs Valley region. What began as a stopover for buffalo and pioneers was soon to become America's premier health resort. The rivalry between the French Lick Springs Hotel and the West Baden Springs Hotel would make the two communities known worldwide for elegance, luxury, and hospitality. A succession of ambitious men with grand plans would transform the valley into a thriving destination. The wonders of the magical mineral waters attracted visitors from far and near.

From humble beginnings as a small rustic inn, the French Lick Springs Hotel was soon expanding to meet the increased demand of guests seeking to improve their health. The original owner, Dr. William Bowles, operated the hotel primarily as a seasonal resort that closed during the winter. After Bowles's death in 1873, the resort changed hands to a series of partnerships, each adding improvements and amenities. The property was eventually acquired by a group led by Indianapolis businessman and former mayor Thomas Taggart. Taggart would soon buy out his partners and become the hotel's sole owner around the turn of the 20th century. His ownership would last nearly three decades, creating a world-class health resort destination that featured golf, gambling, and gourmet dining.

Down the road at the West Baden Springs Hotel, substantial changes were in store as well. Dr. John Lane made many improvements to his basic wood-framed structure. Business increased, and Lane sold the property to a partnership that continued the expansion. In 1888, this group added a partner with monumental ambition and vision, Indiana businessman Lee Sinclair. Sinclair soon bought out his partners and expanded the resort, adding a casino, electric lighting, and steam heat. In 1901, fire consumed the building, and the hotel was a total loss. Speculation was that the elder Sinclair would give up and retire from the hotel business. But the 65-year-old visionary vowed to start over, and a magnificent new hotel arose from the ashes. Designed by gifted architect Harrison Albright, the new West Baden Springs Hotel was soon dubbed the "Eighth Wonder of the World." The structure was guaranteed fireproof and featured a domed atrium unparalleled for its beauty and elegance. At the dawn of the 20th century, the French Lick–West Baden region was poised for greatness. With two major resort hotels, weekly trainloads of guests, and high demand for the curative waters, growth and prosperity seemed unlimited.

Lee Sinclair was a successful businessman from Salem, Indiana, when he bought an interest in the West Baden Springs Hotel in 1888. The charismatic Civil War veteran often referred to himself as "Colonel." He soon bought out his partners and embarked on an ambitious expansion to compete with the nearby French Lick Hotel. Electric lighting and steam heat were added, along with an opera house, natatorium, and regular rail service from St. Louis. (Courtesy of Suzanne Emmons.)

Thomas Taggart, well known in Indiana politics, was a popular former mayor of Indianapolis. As a frequent visitor to the resorts at French Lick and West Baden, he saw the potential and formed a partnership to buy the French Lick Hotel in 1901. He soon made numerous additions and improvements and eventually bought out his partners to become sole owner. Taggart's political connections and flair for elegant hospitality created a "golden era" at the hotel and established the place as a world-class resort. (Courtesy of French Lick Resort.)

This is the original Pluto Spring House at the French Lick Hotel, as it appeared in the late 1800s. The all-wooden structure had stairs leading up to a mezzanine with benches and railings. The actual spring was accessible from the ground level. The building has been replaced twice. The current pagoda-style brick structure was built in the mid-1910s and is featured prominently today on the resort's logo. (Courtesy of French Lick Resort.)

This view shows the grounds of the French Lick Hotel around 1901. The new century brought significant changes to this landscape. The Pluto Spring House, near the center of the photograph, is the only structure that remains today, but it hardly recognizable after several remodels and upgrades. (Courtesy of French Lick West Baden Museum.)

This is the bowling and billiards pavilion at the French Lick Hotel as it appeared at the turn of the 20th century. The Prosperine Spring House is visible at right. In Roman mythology, Prosperine was the goddess of springtime and the wife of Pluto. (Courtesy of French Lick West Baden Museum.)

French Lick Springs Hotel, French Lick, Ind.

New Health

and a re-kindled joy in existence will be gained by you at

French Lick West Baden Springs

with their marvelous waters, unequaled in this country or abroad.

A couple of weeks at either resort will set you right, if you're all run down. Ideal time to go is now. You can simply rest, or you can have healthful recreation of every kind. Test the curative properties of these waters for stomach, liver and kidney troubles.

Situated delightfully in Southern Indiana. For information, address

FRANK J. REED, Gen'l Pass. Agt.

Republic Building, Chicago.

The original building at the French Lick Springs hotel had a very distinctive roofline, with dome-style cupolas at both ends. These were removed during a remodeling around 1905, as were the mansard-style roof features along the top floor. (Courtesy of French Lick West Baden Museum.)

An early Monon Railroad advertisement for the Chicago market promises guests that "new health and a re-kindled joy in existence" will be gained by a visit to French Lick and West Baden. The Monon operated almost entirely within the state of Indiana, with the main line connecting to Chicago's Dearborn Station. (Courtesy of French Lick West Baden Museum.)

This front view of the French Lick Hotel shows the new 1905 annex addition at left. This was among the first expansions added by owner Tom Taggart after he bought out his partners in the French Lick Springs Hotel Company. Other improvements that year included the expanded bathhouse and powerhouse, plus completely rebuilt the Pluto, Bowles, and Prosperine Spring Houses. (Courtesy of French Lick West Baden Museum.)

Here are a group of carpenters at work on the 1911 expansion at the French Lick Hotel. The new wing added six floors of rooms onto the existing building and was clad in the traditional yellow "French Lick brick." (Courtesy of French Lick West Baden Museum.)

This is the Prosperine Spring, also referred to as the "Beauty Spring," near the north end of the French Lick Hotel sometime just after the turn of the 20th century. This spring produced a warmer, "milder" water than the nearby Pluto or Bowles Springs. According to W.S. Blatchley's 1908 work *Mineral Waters of Indiana*, "The waters are a carbonated, sulphuretted solution of sulphates, carbonates and chlorides of magnesium, sodium and calcium." (Courtesy French Lick West Baden Museum.)

Here are scenes of the lobby/front desk area of the French Lick Hotel around 1910. The intricate designs on the floors were made up of thousands of hand-placed mosaic tiles. These remarkable floors are still visible today thanks to painstaking restoration efforts in the mid-2000s. (Both, courtesy French Lick West Baden Museum.)

This is a view of the courtyard area north of the 1911 addition of the French Lick Hotel. The stone feature on the right is the Lithia Spring, where guests could descend the stairs to dip a glassful of Pluto Water straight from the source. Today, this is near the site of the formal gardens area, a venue for outdoor events and receptions. (Courtesy French Lick West Baden Museum.)

After a tragic fire destroyed his West Baden Springs Hotel in 1901, many wondered if owner Lee Sinclair would retire from the business. But within days of the disaster, the 65-year-old visionary vowed to rebuild his hotel bigger and better than before. And he promised to reopen within one year. This illustration shows his grand plans for an extraordinary structure featuring a huge freestanding dome surrounded by towers, springhouses, and lush gardens. (Courtesy of French Lick West Baden Museum.)

The new West Baden Springs Hotel building was to be an octahedron, made up of 15 sections, each 60 feet long. The building's outer circumference was 1,010 feet. The six floors contained 708 guest rooms surrounding the open atrium in the middle. Each room had a private bath, hot and cold running water, steam heat, and electric lights. (Courtesy of French Lick West Baden Museum.)

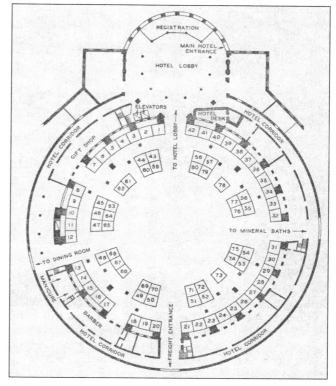

Here, the first floor of the new West Baden Springs Hotel begins to take shape in November 1901. This photograph was taken just five months after the tragic fire destroyed the original hotel. Owner Lee Sinclair vowed to open his grand new hotel within one year of the tragedy. Construction company Caldwell & Drake, of Columbus, Indiana, agreed to a $100 per day penalty if the construction period exceeded 200 days. (Courtesy of French Lick West Baden Museum.)

Construction workers pause for a photograph as the roofline begins to take shape on the new West Baden Springs Hotel. A total of 516 men were hired by the contractor, earning $1 per day for common labor or 50¢ per hour for bricklayers. Fireproofing the structure was important to owner Lee Sinclair. The only flammable materials used in construction were for doors and window frames. (Courtesy of French Lick Resort.)

26

Here, the dome's first steel girders are attached to the central hub, or "drum," on the new West Baden Springs Hotel. Owner Lee Sinclair chose gifted architect Harrison Albright, of West Virginia, to design the unique structure. The plans called for the dome's framework to rest on an innovative system of roller bearings to allow the dome to expand and contract with the weather. Albright was chosen from numerous architects who submitted plans, many of whom claimed the structure could not be built. (Courtesy of French Lick Resort.)

Here, the completed framework is in place for the great dome of the new West Baden Springs Hotel. A curious crowd gathered the day the supporting scaffolds were removed, as there were doubts by many that the structure could stand on its own. Legend has it that architect Harrison Albright demonstrated his confidence by standing atop the framework as the last support was removed and received an ovation from spectators as the structure held. (Courtesy of French Lick Resort.)

Here, craftsmen are assembling the unique Seal Fountain in the middle of the West Baden atrium. This distinct feature was designed by gifted sculptor Ferdinand Cross and sported a water-squirting sea lion perched on a rock. Cross eventually retired to a cabin in Orange County, near a cavern that became known as Cross Cave. It became a tourist attraction, with hotel guests transported there by wagon to watch the artist work. (Courtesy of French Lick West Baden Museum.)

VIEW OF THE WEST BADEN SPRINGS HOTEL, WEST BADEN, IND.

This view shows the completed West Baden Springs Hotel before the major renovations of 1917. The earliest illustrations show the completed hotel with eight towers situated around the central dome, although only half that number were built. The two-story building at right, below the smokestack, housed the natatorium, where the indoor and outdoor pools are still located today. (Courtesy of French Lick West Baden Museum.)

Here is a superb view of the early interior of the West Baden Springs Hotel atrium, photographed by William Henry Jackson before the renovations of 1917. Note the bare brick surfaces on the walls and columns as well as the grand fireplace before the addition of the Rookwood Pottery facade. The original Seal Fountain is in place here, and a string quartet can be seen playing alongside. (Library of Congress.)

This is another view of the West Baden Springs Hotel during a high-water period before the major renovations of 1917. French Lick Creek runs along the east side of the hotel and sometimes overflows its banks during flash-flood episodes. The hotel and attached buildings are constructed high and dry, even though water can sometimes inundate streets and nearby roads. (Courtesy of French Lick West Baden Museum.)

This view shows the east side of the completed West Baden Springs Hotel, with the rounded first-floor grand lobby. This two-story rotunda featured a mezzanine level referred to as the "ladies writing" balcony. In the renovations of 1917, the exterior redbrick trim was painted white, giving the building a "cleaner" look. Also added was a new veranda that stretched from the grand lobby to the garden entrance on the south. (Courtesy of French Lick West Baden Museum.)

Pictured is the new front veranda, added to the West Baden Springs Hotel during the 1917 renovations. Situated on the southwest side of the building, the porch spanned the area between the garden entrance and the grand lobby rotunda entrance to the hotel. It has always been a popular spot to relax in a rocker while overlooking the gardens and the main entry boulevard. (Courtesy of French Lick West Baden Museum.)

Morning Exercise and Base Ball Park, West Baden, Ind.

This is the famous bicycle and pony track at the West Baden Springs Hotel. The distinctive structure featured two decks. The upper deck was reserved for bicycling during daylight hours, then converted to a promenade for strolling in the evening under the electric lights. The lower level was reserved for horseback riding and pony carts. (Courtesy of French Lick West Baden Museum.)

This is the entrance to the bicycle and pony track at the West Baden Springs Hotel. Note the lettering "West Baden Springs Ball Park." The infield area of the structure featured a baseball diamond, and spectators could sit along the upper railing for a good view of the games. (Courtesy of French Lick West Baden Museum.)

INTERIOR OF BICYCLE TRACK, WEST BADEN, IND.

The bicycle and pony track at the West Baden Springs Hotel was built in 1893 and provided one-third of a mile of cycling protected from the weather. The all-wooden structure was unique for its time and very popular with guests eager to have a try at the bicycling craze. The track was heavily damaged by high winds in 1927 and not rebuilt. (Courtesy of French Lick West Baden Museum.)

This is Spring No. 3 at the West Baden Springs Hotel before the renovations of 1917. This wooden building was replaced with a stately stone structure resembling a columned temple. The spring was renamed Apollo, after the Greek god of the sun, music, medicine, and poetry. (Courtesy of French Lick West Baden Museum.)

This Sinclair family photograph was taken not long before Lee Sinclair's death in 1916. From left to right are Charles Rexford (Lillian's husband), Caddie Sinclair (Lee's wife), Lillian Sinclair Rexford (Lee's daughter), and Lee Sinclair. Lillian and Charles would take over management of the West Baden Springs Hotel after the elder Sinclair's death. (Courtesy of French Lick West Baden Museum.)

This is an east-facing view of the rear of the French Lick Hotel, with the Pluto Spring House visible at left. This wing of the hotel was constructed in 1911 at a cost of $400,000 and nearly doubled the room capacity. Yet another building would be added on at the right in 1915. (Courtesy of French Lick West Baden Museum.)

This east-facing view of the rear of the French Lick Hotel shows the 1915 addition, known as the deluxe wing or A Wing. Owner Tom Taggart and his wife, Eva, resided in a sixth-floor apartment in this section. The formal gardens provided an inviting place for an after-dinner stroll. (Courtesy of French Lick West Baden Museum.)

WEST BADEN SPRINGS HOTEL, WEST BADEN, IND.

DINNER.

Friday, June 11, 1915.

Crab Meat Cocktail

Clam Chowder, Boston Style   Consomme, Vermicelli

Dill Pickles   Shallots   Mixed Pickles

Grilled Roe Shad, Sauce Meuniere
Potatoes, Long Branch

Smoked Ox Tongue, Tomato Sauce

Lobster, a la Newburg, in Cases
Braised Young Pig, Apple Sauce
Cocoanut Custard Fritters, au Vanilla

CURRANT SHERBET

Roast Prime Ribs of Beef, au Jus

Mashed Potatoes   Stringless Beans

Roast Turkey, Stuffed, Cranberry Sauce

Potatoes, Boiled   Stewed Kohlrabi

Stewed Tomatoes

Lettuce and Tomato Salad

Baked Rice Pudding, Cream Sauce

Apple Pie   Cream Custard Pie

Vanilla Ice Cream   Assorted Cake

Apples   New Cherries

Roquefort or Swiss Cheese   Water Crackers

Tea   Coffee

Guests using the waters should avoid uncooked fruits, raw vegetables
and all acids.

This is a dinner menu from the West Baden Springs Hotel in June 1915. It featured such delicacies as smoked ox tongue, lobster Newburg and cocoanut custard fritters. Note the disclaimer: "Guests using the waters should avoid uncooked fruits, raw vegetables and all acids." (Courtesy of French Lick West Baden Museum.)

36

The Mount Airie Tower was located on high ground just west of the West Baden Springs Hotel. Postcards proclaimed the structure as the "highest point in the state of Indiana." It was built in the mid-1890s by a man named Ed Buerk, who operated a saloon on the first floor. After an exhausting climb, visitors could see 50 miles on a clear day. When the attraction closed, Thomas Taggart razed the tower and built a stunning new mansion for his son on the site. The home has since been renovated and is now the clubhouse for the Pete Dye Golf Course. (Courtesy of French Lick West Baden Museum.)

An electric trolley line was established in 1903 between the West Baden Springs Hotel and French Lick, and it quickly proved very popular with guests. As a fast and modern alternative to a horse and carriage on a dirt road, the trolley service proved a sensation. In 1916, it set a record for carrying 250,000 passengers in one year. (Courtesy of French Lick West Baden Museum.)

These panoramic images illustrate the profound changes made to the interior of the West Baden atrium by Lillian Sinclair Rexford and her husband, Charles. The space was converted into a Pompeian court theme, complete with statues of Apollo and three of the muses, Calliope, Clio, and Thalia. The 24 exposed-brick columns were coated and smoothed to resemble marble. Twelve

million mosaic tiles were painstakingly laid on the floor in intricate designs. Brick facades were covered with a wainscoting of Hauteville marble. The frescoes of balloons, birds, and airships on the ceiling were replaced with ornate designs to complete the overall theme. (Courtesy of French Lick West Baden Museum.)

After Lee Sinclair's death in 1916, his daughter Lillian and her husband, Charles Rexford, assumed management of the West Baden Springs Hotel. The couple made extensive changes to the property, turning the atrium into a Pompeian court with patterns drawn from Greek, Roman, and Byzantine tradition. Artisans like the ones pictured here installed custom tile and marble over the old brick facades. (Courtesy of French Lick West Baden Museum.)

The Sinclair family coat of arms remains today in the floor of the front porch of the West Baden Springs Hotel. The Latin motto *Aspera Virtus* roughly translates to "The difficult things make us strong," an appropriate sentiment of Lee Sinclair's tenacity to rebuild such a spectacular hotel after the devastating fire of 1901. The full-color design was likely created by the Rookwood Pottery Company, of Cincinnati, Ohio, creators of the splendid fireplace surround in the hotel's atrium. (Author's collection.)

The magnificent fireplace in
the atrium of the West Baden
Springs Hotel was produced
by the Rookwood Pottery
Company, of Cincinnati,
Ohio. Commissioned by hotel
owner Lillian Sinclair, the
intricate design depicts a scene
in the Springs Valley with
Sprudel, the hotel's mascot elf,
perched alongside a cascade
of healing mineral waters. He
is drinking from a ram's horn
beneath the branches of a
catalpa tree, and the hotel can
be seen in the far-off distance.
The one-of-a-kind surround
is made up of full-color glazed
pottery pieces and measures
19 feet long and 11 feet high.
(Both, author's collection.)

Here are scenes of early golf at the West Baden Springs Hotel. Guests could choose between a nine-hole course on nearby Mount Airie, or this 18-hole course that teed off just outside the hotel. Both courses were designed in 1904 by renowned course designer Tom Bendelow, affectionately known as the "Johnny Appleseed of Golf." Bendelow is credited with having designed some 600 courses in a 35-year span. (Both, courtesy of Suzanne Emmons.)

West Baden Springs

The Carlsbad of America

West Baden, Ind.

The cover of this travel brochure from the 1910s features a Native American maiden seeking the healing waters of West Baden Springs. This elaborate 40-page pamphlet touts West Baden as "an admirable, all-the-year-round resort. The winters are rarely severe and the heat of summer is scarcely felt in the cool shade of the hills." (Courtesy of Indiana State Library.)

From November 1918 to April 1919, the West Baden Springs Hotel was converted to US Army General Hospital No. 35. The mission of healing and convalescence was the same, but now rather than treating the privileged elite, the hotel welcomed wounded soldiers returning from World War I. The above photograph shows a band made up of hospital patients posing in the newly renovated atrium. (Both, courtesy of French Lick West Baden Museum.)

Pictured are nurses posing at the West Baden Springs Hotel during the Army hospital years of 1918 to April 1919. The photograph at right shows the chapel of Our Lady of Lourdes Catholic Church, which was located behind the hotel to the west. The church was built by hotel owner Lee Sinclair as a convenience to his guests, but the structure was dismantled in 1934 when it was determined to be in an unsafe condition. (Both, courtesy of French Lick West Baden Museum.)

As part of the 1917 renovations at the West Baden Springs Hotel, the iconic Seal Fountain was moved from the center of the atrium to the roundabout intersection of West Baden Avenue and Geneva Street, near the sunken gardens. It was apparently removed by the Jesuits during the period they owned the property. Efforts to recover the statue over the years have turned out to be fruitless. Fans of West Baden relics consider the seal to be the holy grail of West Baden collectibles. (Courtesy of French Lick West Baden Museum.)

West Baden's Spring No. 7, later named Sprudel, was housed in this elaborate brick structure built during the 1917 renovations. It replaced an all-wooden pagoda-style building. This prolific spring had an estimated capacity of nearly 2,000 barrels per day, enabling a bottling operation similar to the Pluto Water of French Lick. (Courtesy of French Lick West Baden Museum.)

This new building for Spring No. 1 at West Baden was built of brick and limestone during the 1917 renovations. It was renamed the Hygeia spring, after the Greek goddess of health. Located on the west side of the sunken garden, the structure is still in place today, although the spring was capped by the Jesuits because it was prone to flooding. (Courtesy of French Lick West Baden Museum.)

Three

THE WORLD COMES TO VISIT

American history refers to 1890s–1920s as the Progressive Era, with an emphasis on "good health and clean living." The water that poured forth from the ground in the Springs Valley region brought promises of vigor and vitality. The French Lick and West Baden Springs Hotels both created their own "house brands" of the sulfur-rich water. French Lick named their product Pluto Water, in honor of the Roman god of the underworld. West Baden trademarked the name Sprudel Water, borrowing the German word for "spring." Marketing efforts featured mascots, testimonials, and recommendations for daily intake. Doctors' endorsements were common. Many guests were sent to French Lick or West Baden on orders from a physician for a week of activity, healthy food, and "water treatments." Such a regimen was prescribed to treat such disorders such as dysentery, dyspepsia, pimples, insomnia, hives, malaria, rheumatism, and gout.

The two major hotels were competing for visitors, adding features and amenities that rivaled the world's greatest resorts. At West Baden, guests could relax under palm trees inside the great domed atrium or enjoy a round of golf on their choice of two courses. Bicycling was all the rage, and West Baden guests could ride on a covered, double-decker, wooden track on the hotel grounds. Down the road at the French Lick Hotel, enhancements included renovation of the original hotel and the addition of four connected wings. The new west wing featured an elaborate Renaissance Revival–style pavilion, originally named the Pluto Bar. Horseback riding, bowling, billiards, a gym, and a Japanese garden were among the added features at French Lick.

Gambling was big business in the Springs Valley during this period. At one time, there were at least nine casinos operating in the area, some with their own hotel rooms. Others were called supper clubs or nightclubs and offered entertainment along with the casino games. Since gambling was technically illegal in the state, these casinos sometimes attracted a certain criminal element. Rumors tell of visits by underworld notables such as Al Capone and Diamond Jim Brady. But as the Roaring Twenties drew to a close, profound changes were in store for the fortunes of the Springs Valley resorts and their guests. The stock market crash of 1929 and the Great Depression ushered in an era of decline and hard times that would endure for over 30 years.

The grand entry archway beckoning guests to the West Baden Springs Hotel proclaims it as the "Carlsbad of the West." This refers to the spa town of Karlovy Vary (German translation "Carlsbad"), situated in western Bohemia, Czech Republic. World famous for its warm springs, Karlovy Vary was popular with the elite of the European artistic and cultural community. (Courtesy of French Lick West Baden Museum.)

This photograph shows the exterior of the West Baden Springs Hotel after the renovations of 1917. The building has a "cleaner" look, as the exposed redbrick trim has been painted white. The new veranda/front porch is visible on the lower right. This feature soon proved very popular with guests eager to pass the time in the rocking chairs with a fine view of the recently renovated Sunken Gardens. (Courtesy of French Lick West Baden Museum.)

The steel framework of the dome at the West Baden Springs Hotel was considered an engineering marvel when it opened in 1902. It claimed the title of largest free-spanning dome in the world, exceeded by the 1955 opening of Charlotte Coliseum in North Carolina. The 24 steel-rib girders weigh four and a half tons each. They are mounted on columns by a unique roller-bearing system. This allows the roof to expand and contract with the variable Indiana weather conditions. (Both, courtesy of French Lick West Baden Museum.)

Here is a detailed photograph of the ceiling's medallion feature in the dome of the West Baden Springs Hotel. This was added during the 1917 renovations to hide the hub's central drum structure. Some old-timers insist the medallion could be lowered by cables, creating a suspended stage for a band or orchestra. No photographs exist of such a configuration, and a recent inspection of the medallion revealed no evidence such a mechanism was ever in place. (Courtesy of French Lick West Baden Museum.)

"The Home of Pluto Water"

French Lick Springs Hotel, French Lick, Ind.

This postcard image shows the French Lick Hotel around 1930. The resort's various wings and additions were added in 1905, 1911, 1915, and 1925. This basic "footprint" of the hotel would remain unchanged until the addition of the new conference center and casino in 2006. (Courtesy of French Lick West Baden Museum.)

Formal Gardens French Lick Springs Hotel, French Lick, Ind.

These formal gardens were located at the rear of the French Lick Hotel and featured elaborate lawns and manicured hedges. Guests were encouraged to take leisurely walks as part of their daily health regimen. Owner Thomas Taggart proclaimed, "The gardens are as good for your soul as the Sulphur baths for your aches and pains." (Both, courtesy of French Lick West Baden Museum.)

"The Home of Pluto Water"

Park Entrance, French Lick Springs Hotel, French Lick, Ind.

These are views of the exterior of the "Hot Pluto Buffet" at the French Lick Hotel. Located adjacent to the garden area, the bar inside served hot and cold Pluto Water to guests without them ever having to step outdoors. The stone face of Pluto, Roman god of the underworld, is featured in the building's ornate trim work. (Both, courtesy of French Lick West Baden Museum.)

This image shows the rear of the French Lick Hotel and exterior of the "Hot Pluto Buffet." This elaborate structure featured a walk-up bar with hot and cold running Pluto Water. Note the two statues on the roof of Pluto, god of the underworld. In the foreground is the Lithia Spring, the only one of the four original springs never enclosed with a springhouse structure. (Courtesy of French Lick West Baden Museum.)

This is an interior view of the "Hot Pluto Buffet" at the French Lick Hotel. Located not far from the lobby, it provided guests with convenient access to Pluto Water. Otherwise, drinkers wishing to "take the waters" would need to walk to one of the four outdoor springs and dip out the water with a long-handled goblet. (Courtesy of French Lick West Baden Museum.)

These guests are enjoying a drink of Pluto Water from the Pluto Spring, located not far from the hotel near the Japanese garden. The water was accessed by means of dipping a glass goblet attached to a wooden handle. Doctor recommendations often prescribed multiple glassfuls of the sulfur-rich water before meals and near bedtime. (Both, courtesy of French Lick West Baden Museum.)

The French Lick Hotel's water featured a brand name and a mascot. Pluto Water was named for the Roman god of the underworld, a reference to the water's subterranean source. The product's laxative properties came from a high content of mineral salts, with the active ingredients listed as sodium and magnesium sulfate, producing results generally within one hour of ingestion. This prompted the tagline, "When Nature Won't, Pluto Will," often answered with the sarcasm "When Pluto Won't, Make Your Will." (Both, courtesy of French Lick West Baden Museum.)

Demand for the product increased, so a bottling plant was added. Pluto Water was shipped out of the valley on the Monon Railroad to customers nationwide. By 1919, a total of 450 boxcar loads were shipped out annually, in custom freight cars featuring the red devil logo. Doctors and druggists were supplied with free samples, and the product was advertised in national magazines. (Both, courtesy of French Lick West Baden Museum.)

A group of French Lick Hotel guests visit one of the springs with Yarmouth Wiggington, popularly known as "Mr. Pluto." The resort characterized Wiggington as "a respected member of the African-American community" and leader of the Knights of Pythias Lodge, in addition to portraying the god of the underworld. He is buried in the black section of the Mount Lebanon Cemetery in French Lick. (Both, courtesy of French Lick West Baden Museum.)

Here is the familiar green bottle of Pluto Concentrated and Fortified Spring Water featuring an illustration of the French Lick Hotel and the "God of the Underworld" devil mascot. The label declares the active ingredients are sodium sulfate and magnesium sulfate. Modern analysis also revealed traces of lithium, which is a controlled substance. For this reason, the public springs were sealed in the 1970s. (Courtesy of French Lick West Baden Museum.)

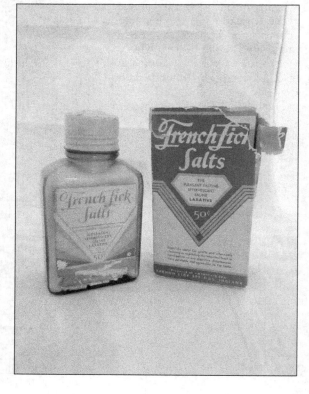

This bottle of French Lick Salts was to be mixed with ordinary water at home to produce a "pleasant-tasting, effervescent saline laxative . . . for gently and effectively cleansing or regulating the intestinal tract." Advertisements stated the product was effective from a half hour to two hours after ingestion. (Courtesy of French Lick West Baden Museum.)

This child's game promotes the sale of French Lick Pluto Water by doctors and druggists. The name "America's Greatest Physic" was trademarked by owner Tom Taggart in 1901 with Indiana's secretary of state. Also trademarked were the names "Pluto," "Pluto Concentrated," and the likeness of the devil for the purposes of marketing the water worldwide. (Courtesy of French Lick West Baden Museum.)

The French Lick Hotel lays claim to being the birthplace of tomato juice. Legend has it that on a morning in 1917, chef Louis Perrin discovered he was out of oranges to make juice for breakfast in the French Lick kitchens. He had an abundance of tomatoes on hand, so he hastily concocted a new drink he simply called tomato juice. His guests approved, and soon the new beverage gained popularity throughout the land. (Courtesy of French Lick West Baden Museum.)

Sprudel Water was the brand name given to the mineral water at West Baden Springs Hotel. Guests followed sidewalks to several numbered springs on the property, all housed in various shelters. The resort's marketing featured an elf named "Sprudel," named after the German word for "spring." (Both, courtesy of French Lick West Baden Museum.)

Spring No. 7,
West Baden Springs, Ind.

Pictured here are relaxing scenes on the spacious front porch of the French Lick Hotel. From this vantage, guests can observe the comings and goings of visitors to the resort's front door—a pastime as popular today as it was 100 years ago. (Both, courtesy of French Lick West Baden Museum.)

This is the gentlemen's indoor swimming pool and changing room area at the French Lick Hotel. Separate from the smaller ladies' pool, both pools featured separate bath areas and changing rooms. Elegant stained-glass skylights allowed filtered sunlight in during the day. (Both, courtesy of French Lick West Baden Museum)

These ladies are happily enduring the confines of a steam-bath treatment in the spa at the French Lick Hotel. This conditioning promised to "soothe the nerves, open the pores, and drive poisons out of the blood." The women's bath department also featured hairdressing, manicures, and various medicinal baths. (Courtesy of French Lick West Baden Museum.)

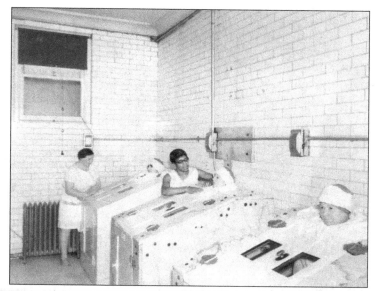

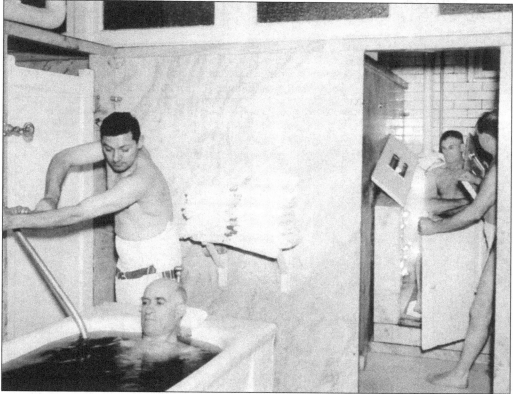

The grim expression on the bather's face suggests a rich sulfur aroma was coming from his bathwater at the French Lick Hotel. When a guest made an appointment, he was assigned an attendant to assist with the bath or massage. Guests could choose from Turkish, Russian, or "Electric Light" baths. Also available were rubdowns with salt, alcohol, cocoa butter, and oil. (Courtesy of French Lick West Baden Museum.)

Here is the height of luxury in early 20th century—a room at the elegant West Baden Springs Hotel. The suites were appointed with the finest Victorian furniture of the day. The domed atrium is visible through the open windows. The 708 rooms featured steam heat, phones, private bath, hot and cold running water, and electric lights. (Courtesy of French Lick West Baden Museum.)

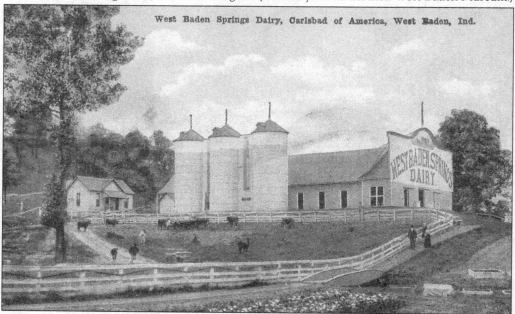

To ensure its chefs had the freshest milk, cheese, and butter, the West Baden Springs Hotel operated a dairy not far from the kitchen door. The French Lick Hotel also operated a dairy. The farm even bottled and labeled surplus milk for retail under the brand name Springs Valley Dairy. (Courtesy of French Lick West Baden Museum.)

A low, marshy area behind the French Lick Hotel was transformed into a delightful Japanese garden. Guests would enjoy the quiet solitude after a visit to the nearby Pluto Spring. The garden is still popular with guests today and is adjacent to the Clifton Terrace, a popular venue for weddings. (Courtesy of French Lick West Baden Museum.)

Local businessman Ed Ballard bought the West Baden Springs Hotel from Lillian and Charles Rexford in 1923. Ballard had learned the hotel business from Lillian's father, Lee Sinclair, and had a string of successes with casinos, saloons, and a circus. The Rexfords were financially in debt to Ballard for the hotel's lavish renovations of 1917. For years, Ballard had fostered a private ambition to own the hotel. Little did he know that in less than 10 years he would be forced to close the hotel and sell the property for only $1. (Courtesy of French Lick Resort.)

Twenty-Third Con
French Lick

The 1931 Democratic Governors Conference was held at the French Lick Hotel with 23 governors in attendance. It was here that New York governor Franklin D. Roosevelt (front row, 13th from left) gathered support for his party's presidential nomination. While Thomas Taggart served as

ence of Governors
June 1-3, 1931

national Democratic Party chairman prior to his death, his hotel developed a reputation as the unofficial national party headquarters. Roosevelt secured the presidential nomination at the party's convention in Chicago the following year. (Courtesy of French Lick West Baden Museum.)

The circus comes to town! This extraordinary photograph shows a circus parade proceeding west on West Baden Avenue in front of the hotel. The big top tents are set up in the meadow on the north side of the street in this scene from the 1930s. In addition to Ed Ballard's Hagenbeck-Wallace Circus, other shows called West Baden home from time to time, including the Gentry Brothers Circus and the John Robinson Circus. (Courtesy of French Lick West Baden Museum.)

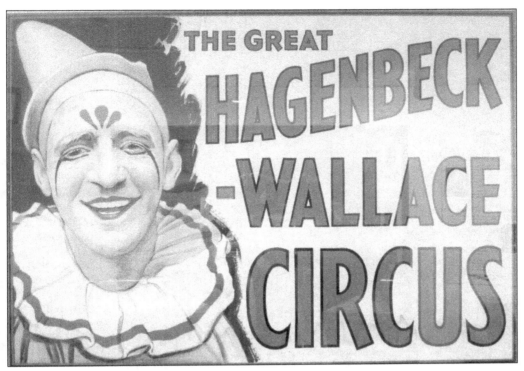

Indiana businessman Ed Ballard owned many other interests in addition to the West Baden Springs Hotel. In 1915, he bought out his partners with the Hagenbeck-Wallace Circus and moved the headquarters to West Baden. This provided the town with a colorful landscape of circus tents and wagons when the show was not on the road. (Both, courtesy of French Lick West Baden Museum.)

Ed Ballard's toddler son Chad poses with a trio of cute cubs from his father's Hagenback-Wallace Circus. In the photograph below, it appears a ferocious tiger is being transferred between an enclosure building and a circus wagon in West Baden. During winter layovers, guests at the West Baden Springs Hotel were occasionally treated to a free circus performance inside the domed atrium. (Both, courtesy of French Lick West Baden Museum.)

GORGE INN, FRENCH LICK, INDIANA.

Many other hotels, nightclubs, and casinos sprung up in the valley during the heydays of travel and tourism. The Gorge Inn was built by businessman George Ham in a secluded valley about a mile from French Lick. Originally a restaurant only, new ownership in the 1920s established the place as a very popular casino. Once gambling was officially outlawed in the valley, the Gorge Inn became a retreat center and later a nursing home. It was lost to fire in 2017. (Both, courtesy of French Lick West Baden Museum.)

FRONT ENTRANCE GORGE INN, FRENCH LICK, IND.

123938

THE FAIR STORE, WEST BADEN, IND.

Another example of distinctive West Baden architecture was the Fair Store, located just across the tracks from the West Baden depot. The unique twin-turreted building was within walking distance of the West Baden Springs Hotel. The Fair Store's selections of fashion and goods were more expensive than those usually found in an Indiana town. The building's basement housed the Kentucky Club, a popular spot for illicit gambling. (Courtesy of French Lick West Baden Museum.)

Prior to 1908, a casino was operated by Al Brown on the grounds of the French Lick Hotel. Thomas Taggart, the new owner of the hotel, was intolerant of gambling, and he put an end to the operation. Brown moved the casino across the street to a luxurious new building he called Brown's Hotel. He built it of the same yellow brick as the French Lick Hotel, much to Taggart's displeasure. Gambling continued at the Brown until 1949. The building was razed in the 1960s and is the site of the Town Green today. (Both, courtesy of French Lick West Baden Museum.)

The Colonial Country Club, seen above, was later known as the Hoosier. It was one of many popular spots for gambling in West Baden. Below, the Southern Hotel proudly advertises "Hot and Cold Pluto" for its guests, even though Pluto Water was a trade name created exclusively by the French Lick Hotel. (Both, courtesy of French Lick West Baden Museum.)

Horseback riding has long been a popular pastime at both the French Lick and West Baden Springs Hotels, one of many activities to enjoy during a visit. Some early guests made extended stays at the resorts, often checking in for weeks at a time. It was common to find well-heeled visitors arriving for the Kentucky Derby in early May and not departing until after the Indianapolis 500 nearly a month later. (Both, courtesy of French Lick West Baden Museum and Suzanne Emmons.)

A major milestone in the history of the towns of French Lick and West Baden happened in March 1886, when Indiana's Monon Railroad bought up two local lines, providing rail links to visitors from across the country. The West Baden Depot was conveniently located within walking distance of the hotel. Wealthy travelers from cities like Indianapolis, Louisville, Chicago, Detroit, and St. Louis routinely made their way here via the Monon line. (Both, courtesy of French Lick West Baden Museum.)

Indiana's Monon Railroad aggressively promoted the features of the French Lick and West Baden resorts with print advertising in Midwest newspapers. The railroad's name comes from the convergence of its main lines in Monon, Indiana. The Monon was merged into the Louisville & Nashville Railroad in 1971. (Courtesy of French Lick West Baden Museum.)

Indulge in your favorite RECREATION—Golf —tennis—horseback-riding—driving—billiards —trap-shooting—bowling—loafing—at

French Lick
West Baden Springs

Two weeks of do as you please and the famous Spring waters will "make you over." The waters are the best in the world for Kidney, Liver and Stomach Troubles. Beautifully situated in Southern Indiana on the

MONON ROUTE

Write for descriptive booklet, rates, etc.

CHAS. H. ROCKWELL   FRANK J. REED
Traffic Manager   Gen'l Passenger Agent
Custom House Place, CHICAGO

An indoor golf exhibition was held within the atrium at the West Baden Springs Hotel sometime after the renovations of 1917. The vast floor space proved perfect for large conventions and trade shows. During 1925, groups such as the Master Plumbers Association, Funeral Directors Association, United Roofing Contractors Association, and Kappa Alpha Theta all held conventions here. (Courtesy of French Lick West Baden Museum.)

The first golf course for French Lick was conveniently located just behind the hotel. Officially named the French Lick Springs Hotel Golf Links, it soon became known simply as the "Valley Course." Designed by Tom Mendelow, known as the "Johnny Appleseed of Golf," the course has been modified several times to have 9 or 18 holes. Mendelow also designed a valley and hill course for the neighboring West Baden Springs Hotel. (Both, courtesy of French Lick West Baden Museum.)

In 1917, Thomas Taggart hired noted designer Donald Ross to create a championship golf course for the French Lick Hotel. Now referred to as the Donald Ross Course, it is situated on high ground about two miles southwest of the hotel. Ross, born in Dornoch, Scotland, was credited with designing or modifying nearly 400 courses over his lifetime. (Both, courtesy of French Lick West Baden Museum.)

Country Club, French Lick Springs Hotel, French Lick, Ind. "The Home of Pluto Water" 124153

The original clubhouse at the Donald Ross Course was a luxurious structure with lockers for over 200 golfers. It contained 30 sleeping rooms, a spacious wraparound porch, and a large living room with a fireplace. The building burned in 1939 and was replaced by the current structure. Several significant tournaments were held on the course, including the PGA Championship in 1924 and the Ladies Professional Golf Association (LPGA) Championship in 1959 and 1960. (Both, courtesy of French Lick West Baden Museum.)

FRENCH LICK SPRINGS HOTEL

This photograph was taken inside the French Lick golf pro shop sometime in the mid-1930s. Advertisements on the wall for the "Pluto 50" golf ball confirm that nearly anything would sell better if endorsed by the god of the underworld. The advertisement proclaims the Pluto 50 as "an amazingly long and tough ball for its price." (Courtesy of French Lick West Baden Museum.)

The French Lick Hotel was one of many US resorts frequented by the traveling elite of the 1920s. The Breakers in Palm Beach, Florida; the Greenbrier in White Sulphur Springs, West Virginia; the Grand Hotel on Mackinac Island, Michigan; and the Cataract Hotel in Niagara Falls, New York, all posted advertisements like this one in national magazines. One traveler was overheard saying, "In the spring we go to the Falls; in the fall we go to the Springs." (Courtesy of Suzanne Emmons.)

Participants in the 1924 PGA Championship pose in front of the clubhouse at French Lick's Donald Ross Course. Legendary golfer Walter Hagen won the tournament, his second of five PGA

Championship victories. Hagen defeated British golfer Jim Barnes in the final round. Barnes was PGA champion in 1916 and 1919. (Courtesy of French Lick West Baden Museum.)

Guests arriving at the French Lick Hotel were given these stickers to apply to their luggage, featuring the famous figure of Pluto, the hotel mascot. Such decals were a tradition among well-heeled travelers of the day. Suitcases and steamer trunks emblazoned with colorful emblems were a source of pride among the travelling elite, showing off all the far-flung destinations they have visited. (Courtesy of French Lick West Baden Museum.)

Four

DECLINING FORTUNES

On Tuesday October 29, 1929, the mood at the stock exchange of Logan & Bryan was grim. Located on the first floor of the West Baden Springs Hotel, guests gathered there in silence as the ticker tape brought news of the stock market collapse. Within hours, the registration desk was crowded with guests eager to check out. In four days, the resort was empty.

The Depression brought an abrupt end to the high-living hijinks of the Roaring Twenties. Extended stays at lavish resorts were now an extravagant luxury as the nation tightened its collective belt.

The French Lick Hotel's charismatic owner Tom Taggart did not live to see the effects of Black Tuesday on his beloved resort. He died in March 1929, leaving his son in charge to meet the challenges of the Depression era. Convention business and golf brought visitors back to the hotel. A succession of owners followed, including the Sheraton Corporation from the 1950s to the 1970s. The various owners made necessary improvements, but by the 1990s, the historic property needed a major makeover.

At West Baden Springs Hotel, prospects were dim as the country slipped into the Great Depression. Lillian and Charles Rexford, Lee Sinclair's daughter and son-in-law, had assumed management of the resort upon Sinclair's death in 1916. The couple made significant improvements, incurring a great deal of debt to businessman Edward Ballard. Ballard bought the hotel in 1922, and business increased under his management. But the stock market crash began a downward spiral resulting in the hotel's closing in 1932. Ballard conceded the property's days as a resort were over, and in 1934, he donated the hotel to the Society of Jesus (Jesuits), who converted it into a seminary named West Baden College. Extravagant furnishings were replaced with less-worldly trappings more befitting the austere Jesuit order. The Jesuits sold the property in 1966, and it was converted into Northwood Institute, a private, coeducational college founded in Michigan. Northwood operated until 1983, when the property was sold to a developer with intent of reopening it as a hotel. Investors failed, and the empty building's ownership was tied up in litigation for nearly a decade. By the mid-1990s, the once grand structure was literally crumbling due to lack of upkeep and maintenance. One by one the valley's other clubs, casinos, and hotels shuttered due to the decline in visitors. By the late 1980s, Orange County was one of the poorest in the state.

The French Lick Hotel managed to survive the lean years of the Great Depression and World War II by promoting its convention and trade show business. A new wing added in 1925 was called the "Convention Hall," and the first floor contained a large stage and auditorium capable of hosting major conferences. (Courtesy of French Lick West Baden Museum.)

Sales of Pluto Water once supported the French Lick Hotel but declined significantly during the Great Depression. Alternative marketing methods, like this mobile sampling unit, sent water sales climbing throughout the 1930s. But the onset of World War II saw decreased demand, and this ultimately forced the hotel to stand on its own to be profitable. (Courtesy of French Lick West Baden Museum.)

Indiana's Monon Railroad laid down tracks almost to the French Lick Hotel's front door. As many as 12 trains per day brought guests to the valley from cities far and near. Parallel tracks allowed multiple trains to back up into the hotel's siding, depositing passengers just a short walk from the front desk. Until automobile use became more common, the majority of guests at French Lick and West Baden arrived by train. (Both, courtesy of French Lick West Baden Museum.)

West Baden College, West Baden Springs, Indiana

In June 1934, owner Ed Ballard sold the West Baden Springs Hotel to the Society of Jesus (the Jesuits) for the sum of $1. The hotel had been closed since June 1932, a victim of the Great Depression and America's changing values. Ballard's generous act of philanthropy was hailed across the nation as the Jesuit order settled into their new home. The hotel's days of excess and high times were over, as the priests began to transform the worldly resort into a tranquil and reclusive religious university. (Courtesy of French Lick West Baden Museum.)

The Jesuits named their new facility West Baden College and set about changing the luxurious resort into an austere and modest religious university. Gone were the trappings of wealth and prosperity, replaced by plain and simple furnishings more befitting of the Jesuit order. The grand lobby was converted to a chapel with pews and an altar. The vast atrium space was considered too immense for the purpose. (Courtesy of French Lick West Baden Museum.)

A significant change made by the Jesuits at West Baden was the removal of the four giant Moroccan towers and decorative trim along the top edge of the building. This gave the building an institutional look that was more consistent with the austerity of the Jesuit order. Once filled with sounds of laughter and frivolity, the halls of West Baden were now scenes of quiet contemplation among the new residents. (Courtesy of French Lick West Baden Museum.)

The St. Ignatius Cemetery is a poignant reminder of West Baden's Jesuit years. Located off Geneva Street near the sunken gardens, it was established soon after the Jesuits arrived in 1934. Thirty-nine priests, seminarians, and brothers who died during their tenure are buried there. To this day, the Jesuit order continues to maintain the cemetery, and some priests still request to be buried there. (Courtesy of French Lick West Baden Museum.)

The French Lick Hotel became known for its tradition of "dancing waiters." Always a crowd favorite, they would carry dessert trays on their heads, entering to the strains of "When the Saints Go Marching In." A newsreel from the 1930s featured a race on the hotel lawn of waiters attempting to run while balancing trays of dishes on their heads. (Both, courtesy of French Lick West Baden Museum.)

For a few years during World War II, the French Lick Hotel was the spring training home for both of Chicago's major league baseball teams, the Cubs and the White Sox. Due to wartime travel restrictions, baseball commissioner Kenesaw Mountain Landis declared that all teams should hold spring training north of the Mason-Dixon line and east of the Mississippi River for 1943. Both teams chose French Lick for the 1943 and 1944 session. In 1945, the White Sox moved training to nearby Terre Haute, but the Cubs stayed at French Lick. Both teams resumed training in California after the war. (Both, courtesy of French Lick West Baden Museum.)

Here is an aerial view facing east of the French Lick Hotel with the Chicago Cubs baseball practice field visible just northeast of the hotel. The town of French Lick is on the right of this photograph. The hotel's dairy farm is at bottom left. This photograph was taken probably in the mid-1940s. (Courtesy of French Lick West Baden Museum.)

Pres. Harry Truman (right) was a close friend of French Lick Hotel owner Thomas D. Taggart (center). During his stays at the hotel, Truman was assured privacy and seclusion by Taggart, a rare privilege for the 33rd president. Other US presidents to visit the resort included Franklin Roosevelt, Gerald Ford, Richard Nixon, and Ronald Reagan. (Courtesy of French Lick West Baden Museum.)

Here is movie star Lana Turner signing an autograph for nine-year-old fan Sally Mitchell on the steps of the French Lick Hotel in 1945. Celebrity sightings were common at the hotel, and Turner was accompanied on this trip by millionaire industrialist Howard Hughes. The actress was famous for her roles in *The Postman Always Rings Twice* and *Peyton Place*. (Courtesy of French Lick West Baden Museum.)

Here are popular comedians Bud Abbott and Lou Costello at the French Lick Hotel during a war bonds tour in August 1942. The two participated in a charity auction, which included the sale of a donkey provided by hotel owner Thomas D. Taggart. The bond tour was a rousing success, earning over $2 million for the war effort. (Courtesy of French Lick West Baden Museum.)

Pictured is professional boxer Joe Louis, World Heavyweight Champion from 1937 to 1949, fishing from a bridge that now bears his name near the West Baden Springs Hotel. The "Brown Bomber" spent a great deal of time in the area and used to train here. He was often seen on training runs around the grounds of the hotels, sometimes joined by little kids racing to keep up with the champ. (Courtesy of French Lick West Baden Museum.)

Pictured is Academy Award–winner and avid golfer Bing Crosby teeing off at the Donald Ross Course while French Lick Hotel owner Thomas D. Taggart looks on. In all of history, it is hard to find an entertainment superstar to top Bing Crosby. In movies, radio, television, and music, Crosby set the standard for talent and showmanship. His 1941 recording of Irving Berlin's "White Christmas" still holds the record for best-selling single of all time. (Courtesy of French Lick West Baden Museum.)

As the age of the automobile dawned, the appeal of personal mobility meant more guests were arriving at the French Lick hotel by car rather than train. The Monon Railroad began running fewer scheduled trains in the 1940s, and regular passenger service concluded in 1949. Some chartered passenger trains, such as Kentucky Derby Day specials, continued until 1971. (Courtesy of French Lick Resort.)

This cocktail lounge was called the Demon's Den, located on the basement level of the French Lick Hotel. It was closed during renovations in 1954, when the space was repurposed into a meeting room. Other improvements during this period included new air-conditioning and carpet, new first-floor cocktail lounge, and redecorated convention hall. (Courtesy of French Lick Resort.)

Here is the modern clubhouse at the French Lick Hotel's Donald Ross Course. This replaced the original structure that burned in 1939. Often referred to as the Hill Course, the Donald Ross Course is located about two miles southwest of the hotel. This clubhouse remains in use today and is home to the popular Hagen's restaurant, named in honor of Walter Hagen, winner of the 1924 PGA Championship played on the course. (Courtesy of French Lick Resort.)

Shooting sports were yet another pastime available to guests at the French Lick Hotel. Skeet, trap, and target shooting were available. Guests could bring their own rifle or use ones provided by the hotel. The shooting facility was located on a hill behind the hotel and offered free lessons for the novice. (Courtesy of French Lick Resort.)

This was the first outdoor pool available to guests of the French Lick Hotel. Located on a hill behind the hotel, it was referred to as the Doll House Pool because it was built adjacent to a small house Thomas D. Taggart built for his daughter Eva in 1925. The doll house remains on property today, although the pool was removed in 2008. (Courtesy of French Lick Resort.)

This unique structure housed the pool at the rear of the French Lick Hotel. Installed in 1965, this dome provided climate control for year-round swimming and could be partially opened during the warm summer months. It was removed during renovations around 2005, when a new pool was built on the south side of the Spring Wing. (Courtesy of French Lick West Baden Museum.)

In 1954, the Cabana Pool was added to the front of the French Lick Hotel when it was acquired by the Sheraton Corporation. While the location was not exactly convenient for the guests, this pool remained in operation until the mid-1970s. Today, this is the site of the hotel's front lawn. (Both, courtesy of French Lick West Baden Museum.)

In June 1964, the Jesuits made the decision to depart the West Baden Springs Hotel for a newer, more affordable domicile near Chicago. Maintenance and upkeep of the West Baden property proved formidable for an order that was vowed to poverty. Some reminders of the Jesuit years remain on the property, like the elegant stained-glass windows in the lobby near the front desk. The lobby had once served as a chapel for the Jesuits, complete with statuary, pews, and a raised altar. (Courtesy of French Lick West Baden Museum.)

In 1964, the Jesuits secured real estate firm W.A. Brennan, Inc., to help find a buyer for the West Baden Springs Hotel. It produced this brochure promoting the property to colleges, corporations, hospitals, religious orders, and hotel companies. The buyer was promised "687 acres of beautiful rolling land . . . adjacent to the famous French Lick Springs Hotel." (Courtesy of French Lick West Baden Museum.)

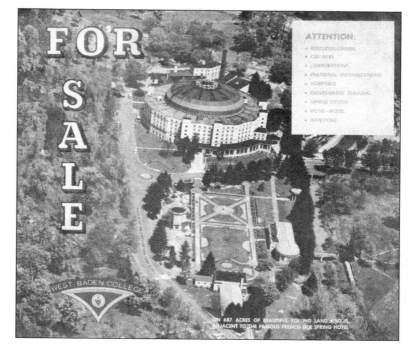

The domed atrium at West Baden Springs Hotel sat empty for two years after the departure of the Jesuits. In November 1966, the property was sold at auction to Helen and McCauley Whiting, of Midland, Michigan, and became home to Northwood Institute's primary campus. McCauley Whiting was president of Dow International and had strong connections to Northwood. He donated the empty hotel to the college, and the property was soon alive again with college students and faculty. (Courtesy of French Lick West Baden Museum.)

Northwood Institute opened its new West Baden campus to students for the fall semester of 1967. The university offered majors in business administration, automotive marketing, hotel and restaurant management, culinary arts, fashion merchandising, and advertising. Northwood claimed to fill a vacuum between liberal arts colleges and vocational schools and enrolled students from two dozen countries. (Courtesy of French Lick West Baden Museum.)

When Northwood Institute moved in, the West Baden Springs Hotel got a fresh coat of paint, plus some sprucing up around the resort grounds. The influx of young college students brought an element of youthful energy to town, with the latest fashions, fads, and competitive sports. This was a major change from the austere, plain, and simple order of the Jesuit priests. (Both, courtesy of French Lick West Baden Museum.)

The above photograph of the gardens at the West Baden Springs Hotel is from the Northwood Institute era. The bowling and billiards pavilion is at left, with the Hygeia Spring House on the right. The photograph below shows a graduation ceremony staged in the atrium in front of the grand fireplace. (Both, courtesy of French Lick West Baden Museum.)

In the photograph at right, Northwood Institute students celebrate a holiday season in the 1970s by decorating a Christmas tree inside the atrium at the West Baden Springs Hotel. Below is a scene of the front entryway during the Northwood era. After 16 years, the challenges of owning and maintaining the historic resort forced the college to close the campus in 1983. Thus, began another period of uncertainty as to the future of the aging landmark. (Both, courtesy of French Lick West Baden Museum.)

In the 1970s, Northwood Institute helped place the West Baden Springs Hotel in the National Register of Historic Places. Suites on the second and third floors were converted to dormitory rooms and separated into areas for girls and boys. Individual plumbing was removed from the rooms, replaced by common bath and shower facilities on each floor. This photograph shows a classic car show being held inside the atrium. (Courtesy of French Lick West Baden Museum.)

Five

RETURN TO GLORY

By the early 1990s, the Springs Valley needed a miracle. The French Lick Hotel was showing its age, and the West Baden Springs Hotel was literally falling apart. Unemployment was rampant, and fires claimed blocks of historic buildings in downtown French Lick. This community that had attracted visitors from around the world was desperately hoping for an economic leg up.

The condition of the empty West Baden Springs Hotel became critical in 1991, when a section of the building collapsed due to ice and water buildup. Historic Landmarks Foundation of Indiana stepped in with emergency repairs, even though ownership of the building was tied up in bankruptcy court. But additional work was urgently needed to save the structure. Indiana had recently approved riverboat gambling, and in 1994, the court sold the hotel to a casino company with the intent of obtaining a gaming license. When the license was denied, the hotel went on the market again. With the help of an anonymous donor, the Historic Landmarks Foundation of Indiana bought the property in 1996. To meet the overwhelming task of preserving the hotel, the foundation sought out a partner with business expertise and financial backing. Bill and Gayle Cook, of Bloomington, Indiana, stepped up for the challenge. Cook was a self-made billionaire with a passion for history and preservation. The Cook family invested an estimated $100 million in the restoration of the West Baden Springs Hotel. After a grassroots effort by local activists, the state awarded the county a gaming license in 2003. The Cooks formed a group that acquired the license and in 2005 purchased the French Lick Hotel, beginning a $35 million renovation there. In November 2006, the newly renovated French Lick Resort and Casino opened to rave reviews. In June 2007, the West Baden Springs Hotel opened its doors and was deemed "The Save of the Century" by preservationists. In 2009, the Cook Group opened the 18-hole Pete Dye Golf Course at French Lick on nearby Mount Airie, converting Thomas Taggart's historic mansion into the clubhouse.

So the story has come full circle. French Lick and West Baden are again home to luxurious accommodations, fine dining, professional golf, and casino gambling. Conspicuously missing from this renaissance are the "healing waters" of the Springs Valley. After expert analysis in the 1970s, scientists discovered the water contained unhealthy amounts of lithium. For safety's sake, the public springs were sealed, a curious footnote to a bygone era.

The Sheraton Corporation owned the French Lick Hotel from 1955 until 1979. The company made efforts to modernize the property, adding air-conditioning throughout the hotel and refurbishing the guest rooms. But to better reflect the era's "mod" tastes, many of the hotel's classic features were deliberately concealed behind drop ceilings, paneling, and wall-to-wall carpeting. Sheraton continued to market the resort as a center for conventions and corporate retreats, with special amenities like golf and tennis. (Both, courtesy of French Lick West Baden Museum.)

Perhaps the most famous native of French Lick is basketball legend Larry Bird, often considered one of the sport's greatest players. He was born in West Baden but grew up in nearby French Lick, attending Springs Valley High School. His mother worked two jobs to support Larry and his five siblings. He attended Indiana State University, where he helped the school's basketball team reach the National Collegiate Athletic Association (NCAA) tournament for the first time in school history. He went on to play in the National Basketball Association (NBA) for the Boston Celtics from 1979 to 1992 and later coached the Indiana Pacers. Bird was the only person in NBA history to be named Rookie of the Year, Regular Season MVP, Finals MVP, All-Star MVP, Coach of the Year, and Executive of the Year. (Both, author's collection.)

The 1980s and 1990s were not kind to the empty West Baden Springs Hotel. After Northwood Institute moved out in 1983, the buildings and property fell into decline, with no realistic salvation on the horizon. In the above photograph, the hotel is no longer visible through the arches due to the overgrown trees and undergrowth. The image below, looking south toward the bowling and billiards pavilion, shows the overgrown foliage in the sunken gardens. (Both, courtesy of French Lick West Baden Museum.)

This photograph from the 1990s shows the deterioration of the bowling and billiards pavilion at the West Baden Springs Hotel. Windows are broken or missing, and vines cover the facade of the grand structure at the south end of the sunken gardens. There was a period in the 1980s and 1990s when the abandoned property was unsecured from visitors. The hotel's isolated location was perhaps its best defense from vandals. (Courtesy of Suzanne Emmons.)

In 1974, the West Baden Springs Hotel was listed in the National Register of Historic Places. In 1987, it was named a National Historic Landmark Monument by the US Department of the Interior. During this time, an attempt by a local developer to renovate the property and reopen it as a resort resulted in litigation with investors in a California court. This created a stalemate that held the property in legal limbo for years, resulting in further neglect and deterioration. (Courtesy of French Lick West Baden Museum.)

These interior photographs of the West Baden Springs Hotel show the dining room area that is today Sinclair's Restaurant. The plaster ceiling is falling, and the standing water indicates a leaking roof. During this period of deterioration and neglect, the hotel earned a place on the National Trust for Historic Preservation's list of the 11 Most Endangered Historic Properties in the United States. (Both, courtesy of French Lick West Baden Museum.)

In these scenes of the West Baden Springs Hotel from the early 1990s, flaking paint and broken plaster tarnish the elegance of the famous domed atrium. This structure was deemed the "Eighth Wonder of the World" when it opened nearly 100 years earlier. Now it was literally crumbling due to disinterest and neglect. (Both, courtesy of Suzanne Emmons.)

During the winter of 1991, a six-story section of the outer rim of the West Baden Springs Hotel collapsed due to ice and water buildup on the roof and drainpipes. This left a pile of brick, plaster, and plumbing as well as many questions about the building's structural integrity. After this setback, the prospects of saving the historic hotel seemed even more unlikely. (Courtesy of French Lick West Baden Museum.)

The partial collapse of the West Baden Springs Hotel in the winter of 1991 drew national attention to the distressed structure and the critical need for emergency repairs. Historic Landmarks Foundation of Indiana (renamed Indiana Landmarks in 2010) stepped in with the necessary funds to stabilize the building. After yet another developer's renovation plans fell through, Historic Landmarks Foundation of Indiana bought the property in 1996 with the help of an anonymous donor. Its plans were to make repairs and find a buyer willing to invest the funds that could save the structure. Tours conducted by the Historic Landmarks Foundation of Indiana allowed the public inside the hotel for the first time in decades. (Courtesy of French Lick West Baden Museum.)

Hard times continued for the citizens of French Lick when an eight-alarm fire swept through the downtown historic district the night of January 7, 1988. Firefighters battled the blaze for four hours before gaining control around 2:00 a.m. Several apartments and five businesses were destroyed, including the Springs Theater. The fire was a disheartening blow to a community beset with a struggling economy, high unemployment, and two aging resorts in need of a miracle. (Both, courtesy of French Lick West Baden Museum.)

Bill and Gayle Cook, of Bloomington, Indiana, were wealthy philanthropists with a passion for history and preservation. They answered the call in the mid-1990s to help save the crumbling West Baden Springs Hotel, stepping in with the money and the vision to restore the structure to its former glory and attract a potential buyer. Cook was a self-made billionaire, starting a medical supply company in 1963 that would grow into a worldwide firm with thousands of employees. When a buyer could not be secured, Cook purchased both the West Baden and the French Lick Hotels and began a massive restoration project that would return the hotels to their former glory. Cook told the *New York Times*, "I got carried away by my passion for it." (Courtesy of French Lick West Baden Museum.)

The long hoped-for miracle that would be the catalyst for the salvation of French Lick and West Baden came when the State of Indiana legalized gambling in June 1993. Thanks largely to the persistent efforts of a grassroots campaign, the state legislature granted the state's 11th and final gaming license to French Lick in 2003. The Orange Shirts were a group of concerned citizens who helped convince state lawmakers of the economic lift a casino would provide to Orange County and of the critical urgency to save the two historic hotels. (Both, courtesy of French Lick West Baden Museum.)

Complex scaffolding goes up in the atrium of the West Baden Springs Hotel in the mid-1990s. Restoring the roof of the great dome meant removing over 230 tons of roofing shingles and replacing them with lighter ones weighing only 32 tons. All skylight windows were replaced, and new lighting was added to the medallion feature in the center of the ceiling. (Both, courtesy of Suzanne Emmons.)

The atrium floor in the West Baden Springs Hotel required significant work to correct chronic cracking and buckling issues. A large area was excavated, and proper drainage features were installed to better handle runoff. A casualty of this operation was the intricate mosaic floor installed during the 1917 renovations. Only about a fourth of the original floor remains in place today. (Both, courtesy of French Lick West Baden Museum.)

Here, construction materials are stored on the atrium floor of the West Baden Springs Hotel during the renovations of the mid-1990s. The amount of construction materials required for the project was quite impressive: 13,000 gallons of paint, over 140 miles of wiring, 7,899 light bulbs, 65,000 pounds of roof shingles, and 19 miles of electrical conduit. (Courtesy of French Lick West Baden Museum.)

These before and after photographs illustrate the dramatic changes to the West Baden Springs Hotel atrium during the renovations in the 1990s. Debris and trash litter the floor in the photograph at right, the result of years of neglect and occasional vandalism. The image at right is a contemporary view with restored marble walls, mosaic tile floors, and period furniture. (Courtesy of French Lick West Baden Museum.)

Considered the "crown jewels" of the West Baden Springs Hotel's roofline, the four rebuilt Byzantine towers were set into place by helicopter on October 24, 1998. Created by a Kentucky company known for building intricate church steeples, the towers weighed 19,000 pounds each. These reproductions were based on historic photographs of the originals, restoring the structure to Lee Sinclair's 1902 vision. (Courtesy of French Lick West Baden Museum.)

In the photograph above, the iconic front entryway of the French Lick Hotel gets a complete rebuild during the renovations of 2006. No expense was spared to bring the old hotel up to modern building codes, all the while maintaining the elegant feel of the structure's illustrious history. The hotel was closed for nearly one year for the extensive renovation. During this time, the Cook family subsidized the hotel staff's unemployment incomes to match their regular salaries. (Courtesy of French Lick Resort.)

This is a present-day view of the newly renovated West Baden Springs Hotel. The extensive restoration project gave the historic structure yet another superlative: "The Save of the Century." Preservation groups worldwide hailed the Cook family and their efforts, which brought this one-of-a-kind structure back from the brink of destruction. (Author's collection.)

This present-day view of the French Lick Hotel illustrates the sprawling additions that have been constructed throughout the years. The buildings at right comprise convention and meeting space added in 2006; the casino is in the foreground. (Author's collection.)

This unique view from directly above the West Baden Springs Hotel illustrates the elegant symmetry of Harrison Albright's audacious design, a 200-foot-diameter circular atrium surrounded by an outer ring of guest rooms in the 16-sided shape of a hexadecagon. This remarkable structure that experts said "couldn't be built" has stood for over 100 years. (Author's collection.)

This is a contemporary view of the atrium at the West Baden Springs Hotel set up for a large social function. With over 34,000 square feet of floor space, dinner seating can be arranged for up to 2,000 people, creating a spectacular venue for weddings, concerts, and presentations. (Courtesy of French Lick Resort.)

This is a present-day view of the casino building adjacent to the French Lick Hotel. Note that the structure is rounded at one end. When opened in 2006, it was originally shaped like a riverboat, complete with a bow, stern, and imitation smokestacks. There was even a shallow, water-filled "moat" surrounding the facility. These measures were in place to comply with Indiana's requirements that all casinos must be "floating." Regulations were relaxed, and the riverboat trappings were soon removed. (Author's collection.)

The French Lick Resort Casino was a key component in the restoration and reopening of the French Lick and West Baden Springs Hotels. Securing a gaming license for the county was no easy task, since the state law only allowed gambling aboard vessels that were floating on a lake or river. A grassroots effort by concerned area citizens convinced state legislators to modify this requirement, allowing gambling to return to the county for the first time since 1949 (and it was legal this time). (Courtesy of French Lick Resort.)

The French Lick Resort's trolley service made a triumphant return in the autumn of 2014. The antique car was lovingly restored by expert craftsmen to resemble the original turn-of-the-century trolley but updated with modern safety features such as hydrostatic transmission and a diesel engine. Guests can ride between the casino at French Lick to a station at the West Baden Springs Hotel one mile away. A ride on the original trolley cost a nickel in 1903; today's trolley rides are free. (Author's collection.)

Perhaps the most significant addition made to the resort by the Cook Group was the spectacular Pete Dye Golf Course atop Mount Airie. Opening to rave reviews in April 2009, the facility was an instant success. The prestigious Senior PGA Championship was held there in 2015 as well as the Senior LPGA Championship in 2017. The course clubhouse is in the original mansion built by Thomas Taggart for his son in 1928. (Author's collection.)

The superb French Lick West Baden Museum is located in downtown French Lick near the Town Green. Many historic treasures are on display here, including a pair of iconic gold statues of Pluto, god of the underworld. These matching figures were originally installed atop the "Hot Pluto Buffet" building at the French Lick Hotel, then later moved to the roof of the front entryway. Some guests were uncomfortable with these sinister effigies, complete with pointed tails and cloven hooves. They were eventually removed but later rescued by the museum, and they remain there on prominent display today. (Both, author's collection.)

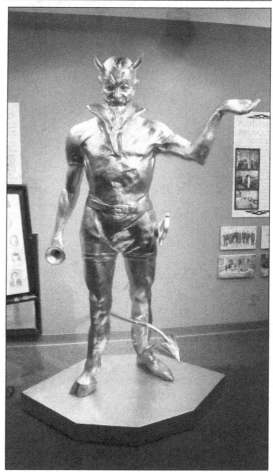

The French Lick Resort hot-air balloon launches from the front lawn of the French Lick Hotel during a summer holiday celebration in 2013. The balloon provides flights for guests and VIPs on holiday and during special occasions. During the 1970s, the hotel hosted a prestigious balloon competition called the Sheraton Cup, attracting balloonists from across the country. (Author's collection.)

An enduring mystery of the West Baden Springs Hotel continues to be the West Baden angels. These figures are found inside the circular drum room on the ceiling of the atrium (see page 26), and no one seems to know who painted them or why they are there. The frescoes are marred by graffiti dating back to at least 1918, but the artwork could be even older. Historians note the figures are faithful to masterpieces of 15th and 16th century Italian artists. Some theorize they could be the work of soldiers convalescing at West Baden when the hotel was a hospital during World War I. Perhaps the Italian artisans who assembled the complex tile floor in 1917 are responsible. The paintings are off-limits to guests since access to the room requires a treacherous climb across the hotel's exterior roof. (Courtesy of Suzanne Emmons.)

BIBLIOGRAPHY

Bletchley, W.S. *The Mineral Waters of Indiana*. W.B. Burford, Contractor for State Printing and Binding, 1903.

Bundy, Chris. *French Lick Springs and West Baden Springs: A Brief History of America's Grand Resorts*. Salem, IN: self-published.

———. *West Baden Springs: Legacy of Dreams*. Self-published.

Gastos, Gregory G. *The History of the West Baden Springs Hotel*. Self-published, 1970.

Longest, David E. *Railroad Depots of Southern Indiana*. Charleston, SC: Arcadia Publishing, 2005.

O'Brian, Patrick. *Pluto in the Valley: The History of the French Lick Springs Hotel*. Martinsville, IN: Fideli Publishing, 2015.

———. *Risen from the Ashes, The History of the West Baden Springs Hotel*. Martinsville, IN: Fideli Publishing, 2015.

Smith, John Martin. *French Lick and West Baden* Springs. Charleston, SC: Arcadia Publishing, 2007.

Visit us at
arcadiapublishing.com

www.ingramcontent.com/pod-product-compliance
Lightning Source LLC
Chambersburg PA
CBHW081600050525
26170CB00030B/44